WITHDRAWN
UTSA Libraries

D1317692

TOBY on the MOVE

By Illa Podendorf

Illustrations by Roger Herrington

CHILDRENS PRESS, CHICAGO

Illa Podendorf, former chairman of the Science Department of the Laboratory Schools, University of Chicago, has prepared this series of books with emphasis on the processes of science. The content is selected from the main branches of science—biology, physics, and chemistry—but the thrust is on the process skills which are essential in scientific work. Some of the processes emphasized are observing, classifying, communicating, measuring, inferring, and predicting. The treatment is intellectually stimulating which makes it occupy an active part in a child's thinking. This is important in all general education of children.

This book, *Toby on the Move,* emphasizes observing the movement of animals. Observations and identification of body structures which make movement possible are stressed.

Copyright © 1970 by Regensteiner Publishing Enterprises, Inc.
All rights reserved.   Published simultaneously in Canada.
Printed in the United States of America

Library of Congress Catalog Card Number: 72-123802

LIBRARY
The University of Texas
At San Antonio

3 4 5 6 7 8 9 10 11 12 13 14 15 16 17 18 19 20 21 22 23 24 25 R 75 74 73 72

CONTENTS

TOBY WALKS AND RUNS

Toby learned to walk
when he was a little boy.
Now he is bigger.

He can walk backward,

and forward.

He can even walk sideways.

Toby can walk faster than
his little sister can walk.
He can walk as fast as his
mother can walk.

Only his father can
walk faster than Toby.

A pony can walk faster
than Toby can walk.
A pony has four legs.
Maybe it walks faster
because it has four legs.

Toby's turtle has four legs.
But Toby can walk faster
than his turtle.

Toby can run.

He can run faster than
his father and his mother.

His little sister cannot
run as fast as Toby.

But his big brother can run
faster than any of them.

No one in Toby's family can
run as fast as a racehorse.

Or as fast as a deer.

Or as fast as a dog.

Or as fast as an ostrich.

Toby can run faster
than his little lamb.

He can run faster than a pig.

He can run faster than a chicken.

TOBY HOPS AND SKIPS

Toby can hop.

None of these animals
can hop as Toby does.

A grasshopper can hop
better than Toby can.

So can a cricket.

Toby can do something
other animals can't do.
Can you tell what it is?
He can skip.
He can skip with a rope
all by himself.

Sometimes Toby can skip
rope with his sister.

TOBY JUMPS AND CLIMBS

Toby can jump.
He can jump the high jump.

Toby's jumps are not as long
as the jumps of a rabbit.

They are not as long
as the jumps of a frog.

And they are not as long
as the jumps of a kangaroo.

Toby can climb a tree
better than many animals.
He can hang from a limb
by his arms.

These animals can walk and run.
But they cannot climb a tree.

These animals can walk and run,
too. And they can climb a tree
better than Toby can.

Both Toby and the baby can crawl
faster than their father can.

This snake can crawl faster
than Toby can.

All earthworms crawl.
But none of them can go as fast
as a snake, or even as fast
as Toby, when he crawls.

Do you think earthworms could
go faster if they were bigger?

This caterpillar crawls, too.
Surely Toby can crawl faster
than it can.

Toby could not swim when he was
small. He had to learn to swim.
He worked and worked.

Toby cannot swim as well as a
fish. He does not have fins
as fishes do.

Toby cannot swim as well as a
duck. He does not have webbed feet
like ducks' feet.

Toby cannot swim as well as a
seal. He does not have flippers.

Even a little tadpole can swim
better than Toby.

TOBY CANNOT FLY

A tern is a bird that
can fly a long, long way.
But Toby cannot fly.

An eagle can soar
high over a mountain.
But Toby cannot fly.

A robin can fly over the barn.
But Toby cannot fly.

Even a chicken can fly
over a fence.

Toby learned to

walk

run

hop

skip

jump

climb

crawl

and swim.

But Toby never can learn to fly,
because he has no wings.

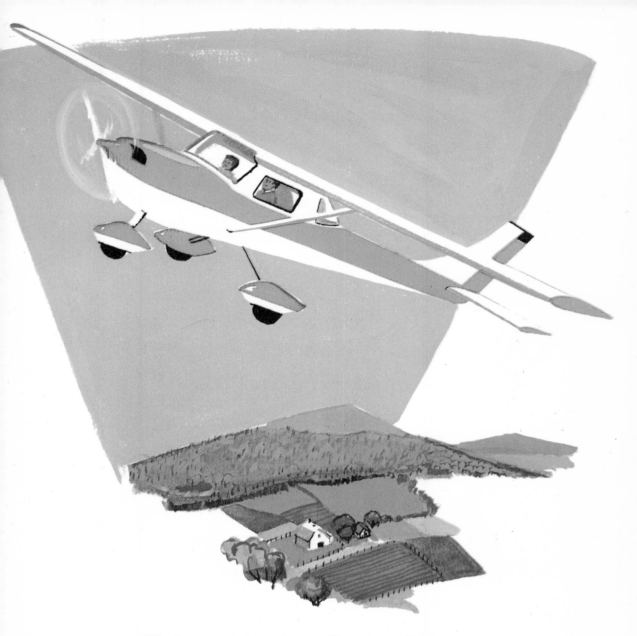

Toby can go over fences, barns,
fields, and mountains in an airplane.

DID YOU SEE?

Did you see the feet
on the walkers and runners?
Did you see claws
on any of the climbers?
Did you see the tail of the
swinger?
Did you see big back legs
on some of the jumpers
and hoppers?
Did you see scales or bumps
on some of the crawlers?
Did you see fins, flippers,
webbed feet, or gills
on swimmers?
Did you see wings on the fliers?

RENEWALS 458-4574

DATE DUE

MAR 24			
MAR 13			
GAYLORD			PRINTED IN U.S.A.